Poet In Our Time

p. 55-56
p. 62
p. 69 - 71
p. 81 - 82

Poet in Our Time

by

Eugenio Montale

Translated from the Italian by Alastair Hamilton

Urizen Books
New York

Originally published in Italy in 1972 as
Nel Nostro Tempo by Rizzoli Editore

© Rizzoli Editore 1972

© This translation Marion Boyars 1976

First American edition published by:
Urizen Books
66 West Broadway
New York, New York 10007

PRINTED IN U.S.A.

Library of Congress Cataloging in Publication Data

Montale, Eugenio, 1896-
    Poet in our time.

    Translation of Nel nostro tempo.
    I. Title.
PQ4829.O565N413   1976b   858'.9'1208   76-21304
ISBN 0-916354-49-0
ISBN 0-916354-50-4 pbk.

Poet in Our Time

About This Book

This book is a collage of notes taken from virtually clandestine reviews, "special issues," literary year books, replies to questionnaires, and written or recorded interviews. With the exception of one or two more recent pieces, these articles were written anything up to fifty years ago. Some of the pieces have also been taken from my book *Auto da fé*, and for permission to do this I would like to thank the publisher Alberto Mondadori.

By and large the material can be considered new if, as has often been said, nothing is as unexplored as a work which has already been published. What is anything but new, on the other hand, is my wavering way of thinking, like a pointer that never pauses either on the white or on the black. My poetic art has always been an assiduous record of a way I have of living "in our time," a time which, to those alive today, seems different from every other time. This, of course, may be an illusion, for I do not think that easy times have ever existed. I have never been able to resign myself fully to chronological time; and it is this congenital diffidence that has always kept me at a distance from any form of integral historicism, whether it be materialist or dialectical. But if I do not believe in the absoluteness of time, I nevertheless have an unshakable faith in the phases that regulate the life of humanity according to a rhythm or a course which eludes metaphysical philosophers as much as it does religious dogmatists. It was difficult to introduce such a feeling into poetry because philosophers and poets play on two different keyboards. Besides, there has been no such thing as a completely rational poetry for many years. If we cannot imagine a didactic poem today it does not mean that the Mind (I use a capital letter reluctantly) is divisible into four segments, or that it is a single entity which operates without leaving any residue in life itself—this would lead to justification, not to say adoration, of all that actually happens, and Italy has provided the most striking example of such a phenomenon.

But let us return to poetry, although it is not the only subject of the following pieces. Poetry differs from prose because it only refers to itself; it can only be explained in its own context, on its own terms. For this reason I have accepted, with neither diffidence nor excessive enthusiasm, the discovery (?) that poetry is a machine made of words and that only these, and the images connected with them, can be studied in their various combinations. I have refused to deduce any hypothetical content from them. Of course the following pages, assembled by my friend Riccardo Campa, are not only concerned with the condition of the poet or the artist in a century of manufactured and artificial objects. They are primarily concerned with the condition of the free man, of the man who would like to be free, or believes he would like to be, in the world and the age in which we are born. I accept the time in which I live. I would not want to live at any other time because today, perhaps more than ever before, it is impossible to believe in an absolute temporal continuity. I do not believe that the days and the centuries have eyes with which to foresee and improve the future. If they ever do it will not be through any fault or merit of ours. In order to illustrate what I call the recurrences of time I have taken the opportunity to publish a hitherto unpublished poem which I wrote after visiting an old Italian garden designed like a chessboard. Whatever its worth, it can serve as an example of my way of *feeling* time.

E.M.

In An "Italian" Garden

The old tortoise hobbles along
its front foot cut off.
When a green mantle starts waving
it limps invisibly into geometrical patches of clover
and returns to its lair.
Since when? An x and the factor
remain uncertain.
For half a century or more. Or back to the times
of General Pelloux. . .
There is no age for the tortoise: all temporal breaks
happen now.

Antella, 3-6-72.

Anyone who observes what is going on around us with a certain degree of detachment must admit that the world is being buffetted by despair and a mysterious, inexplicable love. For example, the monotonous music appreciated by the young, consisting of percussive, repetitive rhythms and immersed in total anonymity, can be regarded as a drugged *amor vitae*, life taken as it is, without predicates. Apart from this conceivable significance of the funereal beat which accompanies us, everything else eludes any justification. It is as though man were discontented with himself, incapable of giving any meaning or content to his life.

It is not for sociologists, theologians, town planners, and Marxists to explain this phenomenon. I, for one, have no personal solution to propose, but when I am confronted by prophets of gloom I put forward a somewhat simple suggestion: I suggest that the world is sloughing an infinite quantity of moral depravities which we of the older generation regarded as sacred and inviolable taboos. But the new skin is too thin, too delicate. It is no longer protective, and will be still less so when the many natural beauties which made life more bearable have been swept away.

The old culture taught us that blind instinct, life in its wild, original state, should be resolutely opposed. But since negation is at the root of every antisocial asceticism many theologians admitted that rigor could be modified by utility. Some went as far as to think that commodities, in other words wealth, were a sure sign of God's preference. But then millions of men arose who thought nothing of all this. With a single stroke they hoped to destroy a way of life which was not only made of paper, rules, and conventions, but which had resulted from the labor and sacrifice of vast hordes of human ants. And would their success have brought about the end of the world? Even if we say, yes, we must add that we can still imagine another world which man can embellish not just with his own hands, but also by the mere fact of living, of existing. I know: we have now taken a leap into the kingdom of Utopia. But were it not for Utopias man would hardly be more ingenious or more unhappy than many other creatures.

Man's tendency to think of man as an end to himself may never have been so strong as it is now. And this is where the root of the problem lies. Millions of human beings long for love, but the word is only uttered in the most sordid realms of journalism.

Newspapers and books, pamphlets and reviews, visions fixed on a canvas or a piece of glass, sounds put together to give us a dynamic impression of physical motion, news and notions showered on us in abundance combine to constitute a vociferous spell intended to inform the lonely man: We are here, too; you are not as alone as you think.

Today an enormous number of individuals want to express themselves, to exist, to burgeon individually. They want to live their own lives on the level which is accessible to them—that of emotions and sensations. And on this level there is no question of privilege: the man in the street has the same rights as the man of distinction and he can even delude himself that his penetration of reality is more authentic than that achieved by the intellectual. But the man of the masses is subject to the ill of the masses, from which none of us can escape.

And the most dangerous aspect of present-day life is the dissolution of the feeling of individual responsibility. Mass solitude has done away with any difference between the internal and the external, between the intellectual and the physical.

Our epoch has substituted excitation for contemplation, and numbers are no longer the secret of divine laws but the subject of statistics. Why, then, should we not draw the due conclusions from the altered living conditions of the man? First he was called *homo sapiens* and *faber* (then *ludens*, and now *destruens*). These conclusions would be to the advantage of the universal nullity which we are on the verge of forming.

What we find in the so-called civilized world (something that has been developing ever since the end of the Enlightenment but is now accelerating at an ever faster pace) is a lack of interest in the sense of life. This has nothing to do with activity: on the contrary. The void is being filled in with uselessness. Man no longer takes much interest in humanity. He is becoming appalingly bored.

For many years now the best artists in the fields of painting, music, and poetry have been basing their art on the impossibility of speaking. Those who speak are the worst artists, the false artists. It is very unlikely that such a state of suffocation can be cured by remedies of a social order or by further neohumanistic disciplines.

The new man is born too old to tolerate the new world. The present conditions of life have not yet erased the traces of the past. We run too fast, but we still do not move enough. In other words the new man is in an experimental phase. He looks but he does not contemplate, he sees but he does not think. He runs away from time, which is made of thought, and yet all he can feel is his own time, the present, while regarding the expressions of the individual feeling of his time as ridiculous and anachronistic. Either he must decide to turn back (and this is impossible) or he must run still faster, in order to benefit from an apparent stasis—that of excessive speed. To run faster means to lighten the burden of his own culture, to break his ties with the old world. It means that he must become a being about whom we do not have the vaguest notion.

It is perfectly obvious that the hypothetical transformation of man into another animal would destroy forever that anthropocentric sense of life which is not only at the root of our civilization but which is also the substance of our way of being and living. Somebody defined the malady of modern man as the progressive loss of a center. This is correct, but it is too facile. To deplore the fact is not to explain it.

Man, the work of man, is a spark of creative energy, and since energy is neither spatial nor temporal, history does not tell us much that interests us, for it only deals with life that is dead.

But to show a preference for energy rather than idealistic reason or the unknown God does not solve any problems: it is merely a change of labels.

In our capacity as men we are affected today with problems of tragic magnitude and with the most spectacular display of mass mechanized life ever provided by history. Who, in the face of this, will be able to justify the fact that the man of today did not react and did not think of hiding and salvaging at least a minimum part of himself? Everything leads us to believe that the man of today is more than ever an alien living among aliens, and that the apparent communication of everyday life—a communication which is quite unprecedented—is taking place not among true men but copies of men.

I do not want to abolish industry, compulsory education, and universal suffrage. Nor do I hope (though I fear it) that some great gesture by the unknown God will annihilate our civilization in a few years or a few hours. This civilization believes it is walking while in fact it is being carried along by a conveyor belt. I do not hope for anything, and I accept the age in which I live. But I would wish that that rare subspecies of men who keep their eyes open will not become altogether extinct. In our new, entirely visual civilization, they are the ones who are in the greatest danger.

At one time, man was believed to be the measure of all things. Later, people continued to regard him as the measure of some things. Today, he is no longer believed to be the measure of anything. Yet the possibilities of the human ant-hill multiply in reverse proportion to the confidence (or loss of confidence) which man has in himself. Some people are gladdened by this, others are grieved by it.

I have witnessed triumphs of human thought which may be prodigious, but may also be sillier than they seemed. I have met heros unaware of their heroism and saints unmentioned in any religious register. I have seen many miseries and many scars disappear, but I have also seen the consolidation of numerous forms of collective servility. And I thought I had discovered one single general rule: every gain, every advance made by man is accompanied by equivalent losses in other directions, while the sum total of possible human happiness remains the same.

I think that the multiplication of branches of science and technology is directly connected with the disappearance of one fundamental idea: that we need not be ashamed of being men.

We see many things die and many others being born, but the meaning and direction of the change elude us.

Nevertheless, our age has the merit of having discovered, or emphasized more than ever before, the total dramatic character of the artistic experience. The endeavor to create works which are the copy of an eternal prototype has been in decline ever since the Enlightenment. Every idea of proportion, decorum, and decency is dead. So the work of today tends to embalm the single, fleeting moment and to make it into something which one can see, touch, and feel. The baser or more insignificant the motive force, the greater the merit of whoever can make it into an object or a substance that will last. The art of today tends to be created for a museum, but not for a museum of fine arts so much as for a museum of fragments, totems, emblems. This produces an art which has no limits and defies all classification. Who will ever be able to write the history of the art of today? Who will be able to produce a scientific history of modern literature? We now proceed on the basis of catalogues and brief records. Some artists still have a name which is remembered and quoted, but anyone who has a name is already living in history, and this complicates matters horribly. The pretensions of these artists who append their names to their products are equally antiquated. In more advanced forms of art, like the theater and the cinema, the name of an author hardly even exists any longer. Ever since the discovery that a work of art is a gesture, it has been more than sufficient for the artist to perform the gesture and then leave it in midair. It is up to the user to identify it and make it his own.

We could add, however, that even if the artists of today eschew the imitation of great models and prefer to parody them, their ambition is to imitate nature in its perennial flux, its continual process of creation and dissolution. The canvas or the sackcloth which has hardly been smeared or singed and *bruitisme* in music appear to suggest something which refuses to be fixed or identified.

The adept of anti-art who has kept abreast of the discoveries of biology, physics, sociology, and economics knows that time is irreversible. He knows that the three-dimensional nature of objects is a provisional victory which has already been outstripped by science, and he also knows that the only reality is the perennial flow of vital energy.

The isolation of the artist (which frequently assumes the form of the most brazen publicity-minded exhibitionism) is inevitable at a time when action and knowledge tread two separate paths and meet only by chance. Distrust of language and the conviction that all bridges have been burnt correspond to vulgarization (in the etymological sense) of the arts. To participate in a collective cry, in a universal *no*, seems to be the sole ambition of the modern artist.

Once the static sense of life has disappeared (the sense that something must hold firm in the *panta rei*), once the diaphragm between art and death has been broken, life itself appears a monstrous work of art that is continually destroyed and always renewed.

What is clear is that the modern popular art to which the aesthetes of today aspire has been in existence for some time and is formed by the mass of audiovisual images which assail us on every side in a way unprecedented before the present century. This mass includes everything, even that which has been defined as art in other times, and whenever we try to make a choice we see the bugbear of art for connoisseurs, and not popular art, raise its head. This is the stage we have reached.

Consequently, once we have entirely discarded the notion of nature, the social structure will have assumed a stable form; the problem of the individual will no longer be felt; history—the history of structures—will consist of accounts and statistics; and art itself, understood as a moral factor, a self-conscious sublimation of perennial primitive instincts, can and must die without remorse.

Within a few decades, the cold war for and against the mass media will appear meaningless. No social revolution will do much to change the techno-mechanical face of the world. Obviously other hypotheses exist, different alternatives, but I do not know if they are any more encouraging. What seems certain is that man will have to pay a high price for his abdication of responsibility.

There is nothing diabolical about the construction of machines. Man is a constructor by nature: he was one when he was sharpening stones and discovering the fusion of metals. The disappearance of the individual, the mechanical organization of life already denounced by the Encyclopaedists and Goethe—a compulsory theme today for a host of journalists—indicate not so much the intrinsic evil of the machine as the ill use to which it is put. The machine in itself is neutral. It is the extension of the hand of man and nothing more.

Such objections to technology collapse if we pause briefly to think about them. What use can be made of the machine in a future ant-hill of human beings who have escaped from an atomic war? What use can be made of travel, sports, cinema, radio, television, illustrated magazines, and strip cartoons when spare time has to be planned and doled out in installments to millions of men freed from the most onerous jobs? How can the instruments of "massification" turn against their inventors and ask to be suppressed?

The optimistic hypotheses are based on the assumption that man remains alien to the machine, that he is not in any way altered by it and that he is in a position to put it to the best possible use. Yet observation shows that the mass-man wants and creates his own destiny and finds the necessary means with which to do so. Mass-produced goods are the basis not only of heavy industry but of the whole new cultural industry which inevitably flourishes at ever lower levels. Once these levels have been reached it will be possible to hope for still lower ones and thereby achieve the hypothetical stereophonic man of the future, incapable even of thinking about his own destiny. And what will then become of man's most useless but most unrestrained activity? What will become of art?

Tomorrow, the number of people aspiring to be artists will have increased prodigiously, because the artistic profession will still be considered attractive and, in many cases, profitable. Tomorrow, artistic production will be still freer, still less restrained, but at the same time it will be ever more conditioned by fashion, by trends, by the influence of critics and cliques, and commercial demands. Tomorrow, too, there will no longer be anyone with the desire or the possibility to learn about technical processes which were once considered indispensable. In other words, the artist of today (especially the artist of the word, the poet) cannot expect acknowledgment or recognition from the future. There will be no room for his work. The entire surface of the globe will be encrusted with artificial products and there will not be a single inch left for anything fresh. Teilhard de Chardin thought that the crust of our planet would become increasingly psychic and that from it would arise a flight of souls. The globe, dispirited, would then continue to revolve in its own orbit, having fulfilled its function.

It is really easier to foresee an immense crust of so-called works of art. Less hard, less indestructible than plastic matter, they can be flung into the oven of history without in any way diminishing the thickness of this crust. Since the capacity of the museums of tomorrow and the ability of the man of the future to take an interest in art have been put into doubt, the artists of today have already started to create their own private museums, thereby anticipating an ever more questionable future glory. There is no lack, indeed there is an abundance, of artists who flee from the problems of the present by creating works which are already prehistoric and cannot be judged individually. This, for example, is the purpose of those writers who claim to anticipate the end of the world. It was the purpose, too, of the futurists, who optimistically celebrated a funeral which may never take place. Gloomier, truer, but maybe less attractive are the poets of the collective neurosis, the breakers of language. Their situation is difficult because the men who should judge them in the normal course of events will not be able to exist in a world which has disappeared.

Our debt to machines is enormous. We only appreciate it when we have to do without them, altogether or even partially: if the electricity supply is cut off for a few minutes, if trains arrive late, if we consider it preposterous that a public organization should constantly transmit the most odious pop music. We do not demand the abolition of electricity, the return of horse-drawn carriages, or even the suppression of state radio and television. No: the inconvenience to which we ordinary men are put when some part of the universal mechanism fails shows that we do not want to dispose of machines, we simply want them to be more numerous, more efficient, and more perfect. In the long run we ask the machine to relieve man of every tiring labor and give him an ever greater liberty. One day, they say, man will be able to work for three or four hours, devoting his spare time to an almost infinite number of leisure activities. But we are already faced with the problem that an immense horde of men obliged to entertain themselves as a social duty becomes a seedbed of fanatics, not to say criminals. And so we return to the eternal problem of the natural man and the artificial man.

It is said that unnaturalness is the destiny of man, having emerged from a state of nature thus entering his artifical phase. *Homo sapiens* still contained a natural, simian element, which must now fade away before the emergence of another being. One day we will have a man made entirely by himself, the creator of his own destiny, the master, if not of his universe, at least of his world. Admittedly the task may last for centuries, but it is worth undertaking. In the meantime, in this age-old antechamber, there is plenty of work for psychoanalysts, psychiatrists, and the cultivators of *un art autre*, a counter-culture, and time alone will mark the final defeat of history.

Man cannot produce a single work without the assistance of the slow, assiduous, corrosive worm of thought. Almost the whole of contemporary philosophy proves this when it affirms that we must live life, not think it, because life which is thought denies itself and appears as an empty husk. We must put something into this husk, no matter what it is. And the vitalism of today, which presumably will be the vitalism of tomorrow within some sort of social organization (either pseudo-democratic or totalitarian), will have to fill the husk in some way, with the minimum amount of time and energy. Therefore industry must be not only cultural but also vital, and sink to increasingly lower levels. And if, in a world of confederate States, immune to every danger of war and class conflict, we actually manage to kill history, the problem of filling spare time will become still more tragic.

But no war can prevent future man from achieving ever more magnificent ends within the limits of an ever more perfect and ecumenical industrial civilization. Any semidestroyed world which arose from the ashes tomorrow would assume, within a few decades, an appearance very similar to the one it has today. Indeed, progress today is being slowed down by a spirit of conservation. If there were nothing left to conserve, technology would advance much faster. Even the large-scale massacre of men and things might prove, in the long run, to be a good investment of human capital. So far we have remained in history. But there is one massacre, that of time, which does not look as though it will bear fruit. To kill time is an increasing concern for the man of today and tomorrow.

So conditioned does man appear to be from birth, so weighed down with every sort of chain, that certain "clerks" or intellectuals think the time has come for him to circumvent the obstacles and emerge from his quandary. We no longer know what to do, they say, with that rudiment of liberty allowed to us which we use in order to make ourselves a seemingly individual niche in the world of production. By so doing we stop at mid-point—no longer men nor yet completely part of a machine. We must take a step forward and turn into machines, consciously and deliberately, even if we are self-propelled machines endowed with some autonomy. We must make a qualitative leap and destroy what remains in us of the old *homo sapiens*. We must not take fright because we do not know where we are going. Anthropology tells us about the man of the past, but it is ignorant about his future. Since man has known how to construct machines which surpass his own mental capacities in many fields, might it not be possible for him to remain in some way man or the semblance of man, but at the same time to make himself into a supermachine more perfect than the others?

What seems to preoccupy philosophers, doctors, sociologists, theologians, and other students of *homo sapiens* is the probable end of man in as far as he is an individual being who claims to express values. The man of today has inherited a nervous system which cannot withstand the present conditions of life. While waiting for the man of tomorrow to be born, the man of today reacts to the altered conditions not by standing up to them or by endeavoring to resist their blows, but by turning into a mass. Eradicating every trace of individual feeling in himself, he agrees to live like an object, concerned solely with preserving his own physical individuality for as long as possible.

A hundred years ago Kierkegaard could write that numbers are the negation of truth. Today this negation has become an intoxicating collective pseudo-truth.

Ideas proliferate, but they are only valid in so far as they can transform themselves rapidly and take off in the opposite direction. It is not a matter of dialectics. Dialectics are an invention of philosophers and they have sometimes been a means of justification for the most abject opportunism. But now the position is different; ideas have become a form of commodity; one puts them on and takes them off at the first change of fashion. A man with a few clear ideas, a man with what are known as firm principles, cannot escape ridicule; and he deserves to be so ridiculed because today all true ideas have been discredited. The fragmentation of technology has also entered the field of moral sciences. For the man who wants to have a successful career, the ideas that count are those surreptitious ones which serve as fuel for the thinking machine. Speed and self-transformation are the characteristics of the marketable idea.

Man is running away from time, from responsibility, and from history.

So far the function of non-art in the world of the future has hardly been glimpsed by industrial designers. It will be to produce perishable and utilitarian objects, works which are no longer subjective but which remind man that he is nothing but energy in a state of perpetual transformation, occult energy which is not beyond us but which is the vital essence of ourselves. The concept of a work which can resist time consequently becomes more anachronistic every day: the work must burn itself out at the moment when it is required and enjoyed by its so-called user.

Natural philosophy or common sense still rebels against the idea that the kernel of man, the essence of man, can transform him radically and turn him into somebody completely different.

But the man in the street is of little importance. He cannot organize himself, and if he could he would become a man of sub-culture. There are plenty of examples. Natural man is the only one who could still concur with Leopardi in deriding achievement. But Leopardi lived in a world which was already progressive and open to the philosophy of light. Recently, however, something strange has taken place: the philosophy of progress has contributed to the development of technology and to the invention of new machines, but in itself, as an ideology, it is challenged far more today than it ever has been before. Listen to the music of today, which openly declares that it is "something else." Look at the sculpture of today: it looks like so many archeological finds, paying homage to a buried civilization. Read the poetry of today: you cannot trust the words since the words are of today, but their meaning must be sought between the lines. The most progressive age that has ever existed has produced an intelligence which avails itself of the new instruments but rejects the ideology which made the age possible. Technocrats are probably unaware of this crisis, since it is merely a crisis of confidence and does not impair the function of the universal mechanism. Everything is made easier and everything becomes more irritating. The forms of escape are few; they are planned carefully, and they are ridiculous. The mere fact of being obligatory and collective turns them into the worst kind of slavery. Illustrious heads of state play golf as "recreation," but when you see that authoritative newspapers devote huge headlines and page after page to occasionally innocuous games of football it is hard not to think that we have reached rock bottom.

We will rise again. But at what price?

Imitation of the divine has become an *imitatio instrumentorum*; if a man accepts the discredited and controversial qualification "intellectual," he quite rightly feels ashamed of it, and all he can do today is to live his period, but remain on the alert.

The God of the physicists cannot even exist in the present, not to mention the future. The idea of God is unique and unrepeatable. Our weak minds cannot help imagining Him as a Person, though not necessarily as a physical person. But in fact He was no more than the achievement of a Condition (perhaps a very improbable one) which matured according to laws of its own, without the Conditioner knowing anything about them.

We might as well admit that such a God does not give any consolation to the human soul, and it was therefore inevitable that He should assume anthropomorphic characteristics. In a mass civilization this sort of camouflage seems to be necessary. The God of our civilization will tend, more and more, to become an object of daily convenience. Of the human attributes we confer on Him He will lose only wrath, not benevolence, and an inclination to compromise.

Since the universe of knowledge tends toward an ever greater totalization of knowledge, it is obvious that it must correspond to an ever diminishing differentiation between men. Of course, the single individual has not yet been completely submerged. Many doors are left open: hence the capillary ramifications of knowledge, and all the new sciences of the human and the unhuman. The thinking individual tries to save himself by filling in the void wherever it appears: the gaps are filled, the exhaust pipes of the knowable closed. So, when the great husk of knowing is full, the immense ball of knowledge will continue to revolve in space, but man will no longer be necessary.

There is still an art which tries to escape from time but nevertheless bears the characteristics of our epoch and consequently supplies far from ignoble material for intellectual entertainment. Yet the potential material of art, the content of art is diminishing, just as the difference between individuals is diminishing.

Our epoch has destroyed art by scrutinizing its nature. It has made art into a copy of something which exists in ourselves and has no need of expression, of "works." Wherever we look we see a rush toward imitation and anonymity, and it would be absurd to expect that when the collective block has reached its grade of maximum solidity the very idea of an individual art, or of any sort of art, should seem anything other than outrageous.

What remains irrefutable is the presence of a universal protest which is not aimed at any particular political or social regime but at our unnatural way of living.

And poetry, which is generally ahead of its time, may go so far ahead as to seem behind in time.

Experience (not reason, that enemy of every impure and contradictory concept) teaches me that there is a universal element in every work of art, but that it makes its way along a path of misunderstandings, translations, and approximations.

The language of a poet is an historicized language or a report. For many years poetry has been becoming more a means of knowledge than of representation. The poet searches for some precise truth, not for a general truth. He wants a truth of the poet-subject which does not deny the truth of the empirical man-subject. He needs a truth which talks of that which u-nites man to other men, without denying all that sepa-rates man and makes him unique.

The subject of poetry which has been most impor-tant to me (the subject, I think, of every possible form of poetry) is the human condition considered in itself, not this or that historical event. This does not mean that we should alienate ourselves from what happens in the world; it means only awareness, and a refusal to exchange the essential for the transitory. I have not been indifferent to what has happened in the last fifty years, but I cannot say that if things had been otherwise my poetry, too, would have changed much. An artist has within him a particular attitude toward life and a certain formal tendency to interpret it according to schemes of his own. External events are always more or less foreseen by the artist, but at the moment when they occur they somehow cease to be interesting. Since I have felt completely out of harmony with the reality surrounding me ever since my birth, this same disharmony was necessarily my source of inspiration.

It is obvious that all real poetry is born from an individual crisis of which the poet may not even be aware. But rather than "crisis" (a word which has become suspect) I would prefer the term "dissatisfaction"—an internal void provisionally filled by the achievement of expression.

The history of poetry is also a history of works which are both great and free. Whether or not it is committed in the sense required by the moment, poetry always finds its response. The mistake is to believe that the response must be immediate.

Poetry, which is half speech and half something else, cannot avoid that unforeseen, contingent element which is man's seal on art and thought. But it is difficult to say how one can apply a principle in which necessity and gratuitousness, the face of history and the face of man, seem to attack and compromise each other at every step, thereby confirming that extraordinary phenomenon: the universal activity of the single man, the infinity of the limited individual.

The poet can build an entire world on a memory. He can organize this memory and apply it to his own particular way of life. But it is not necessary to do all this for art to enter into us and to lead its absurd and unpredictable existence within us. Nor would I ever claim that this second life of art was connected with an objective vitality or importance of art itself. We can face death for a noble cause whistling a tune; we can recall a line of Catullus as we enter an austere cathedral; we can fulfill a profane desire even as we associate it with an oratorio by Handel. We can be struck by one of the caryatids of the Erechtheion as we await our turn at the post office; we can remember a line of Poliziano on days when men run amuck and slaughter each other. All is uncertain, nothing is necessary in the world of artistic refractions. All that is necessary is that some repercussion must take place sooner or later.

There is no phrase of music or poetry, there is no painted or a recounted image which has not taken a hold on somebody, made some impression on a life, modified a destiny, alleviated or aggravated some sorrow. And I maintain that an expression has fulfilled its end and attained a Form if it has had a magic effect on someone, if it has contributed to their liberation or to their comprehension of the world.

A work of art which does not modify our life in

any way, which does not remain in some corner of our memory (even though transformed and disguised), does not exist for us. It is not a living work. But the art of the past has already been sifted: for the art of today we, its contemporaries, form the first sieve, the first experimenters. Let us give the big fish time to remain in the net and the little fish time to slip through the holes. Let us give memory time to perform its first and most urgent task: to forget.

A coarse materialization of the phenomenon of art is at the root of many artistic experiments today. Because of it the artist's second life, his mysterious pilgrimage through the consciousness and memory of man, his complete submersion in life, where art itself found its first subsistence, have been totally misunderstood. I am firmly convinced that a musical arabesque which is not a motif is not an idea because the ear does not hear it as such. A theme which is not a theme because it will never be recognizable, a line or a series of lines, a situation or an image from a novel which can never return to us, however altered and contaminated, none of these really belong to the world of form, to the world of artistic expression. It is this second moment, this moment of infinitesimal consumption and possibly of misunderstanding, which interests me most about art. We could say, paradoxically, that music, painting, and poetry are born to understanding when they are actually presented, but that they do not really come to life if they have no power to continue to act with their own strength beyond a certain moment, dissolving, reflecting themselves in that particular situation of life which has made them possible. In other words, to enjoy a work of art or one moment of it is to find it somewhere other than expected. Only in that instant is the cycle of understanding complete, and art merges with life as all the romantics dreamed it would.

An art which destroys form by claiming to purify it forgoes its second and greater life: that of memory and of circulation on a marginal, reduced level.

Many poets of today, obsessed and sterilized by self-criticism, have as their subject matter poetry itself, or rather the impossibility of writing poetry. This, too, is the case of the meta-novelists who write novels about the impossibility of writing novels. Both seem to be in the same cul-de-sac, forced to perform the inhuman task of involving the reader, since this is "the purpose of the absolute work of art."

It may come to pass that the spirit of History will introduce such elements of confusion, such anachronistic combinations of time into the future boiling pot of art-for-everyone, of standard art, of art conceived as a utilitarian object, of popular and popularized art, that it will cancel out the dreaded uniformity and permit the emergence of the individual spirit, the appearance of those great works which cannot be explained purely in the context of a time or a season, or in terms of a theoretical advance imagined in a sociological sense.

Furthermore, the romantic notion that art is born

from life rather than from already existing art is rarely confirmed in history. We can suppose that it will be confirmed even less in the future. Avant-garde movements (which, when added together, are far more numerous than the traditional ones) are generated by one another and are only understandable if judged in terms of their precursors and of their foreseeable influences. It is a chain from which not a single link must be missing. (Incidentally, when all the links are there, when the classification is complete, we have centuries which are empty, centuries with no poetry. These are the best centuries for the visual arts, assuming, that is, that poetry has nothing to do with the eye.)

It may seem contradictory, but the art which best reflects its time cannot live unless it escapes from its time. History and anti-history play their part in the destiny of works of art, but the poet is undoubtedly born in history and it is not for him to decide whether his work can be understood in another historical dimension.

A work of art may be defined as any expression which solidifies into an object that produces aesthetic satisfaction and that is intended for this purpose (as opposed to the *objet trouvé* which is often more beautiful than any artificial object). If we confine ourselves to this definition there appears to be no reason to speak, as we do, of a possible/probable/imminent death of art. At most we can predict a ghastly increase of so-called artistic production. In the event of so long-lasting a flood, it would be difficult to register and catalogue the immense amount of material and impossible to perform any critical analysis. But we do not have to think about the future. In its less obnoxious forms criticism itself has become an art, and, of course, criticism by artists, the only people who can boast a hypothetical professional competence, has been an art for some time.

I think that the artist's purpose is fundamental to the work of art, although it is not sufficient to give it a value. The artist always imposes something, even if his purpose is not always clear to himself. A work which stops in the middle of the road and tells the user: "We have come so far together, now it's up to you," only appears to require integration. From this point of view the only really open works are the classics, which are fully formed; and century after century we always discover new aspects.

The writer of today knows that the content of his works is subject to rapid wear. Universals no longer interest anybody and only appear in the writings of the few surviving academic authors. What is still of some interest, even if only for a few hours, is a certain type of technique, certain patterns which change from season to season. And the most lasting characteristic of the present time is probably the lack of formal differentiation.

It was inevitable that a new kind of naturalism should come into being in this way. The so-called happening is a rigorous imitation of what goes on in everyday life. It gives us a moment of truth, picked up bodily and cast before our eyes. There is nothing wrong with that: but then it is far more suggestive to go out into the street and watch what takes place. There is now a revival of the beauty (or ugliness) of nature which we thought had been eliminated forever.

Ultimately the true artist is not the poet or the composer of aleatory music, but the man who glances at a page of advertisements or who hears noises in the street and performs the selective gesture of isolating, in that chaos, one moment or one detail which might provide a quiver of vital emotion.

If a work of art is identified with a gesture, no gesture will be able to adapt itself to the infinite quantity of material provided by nature.

We consequently have an art which we look at, no matter whether with admiration or with disgust, but which does not last. The artificial destruction of the artistic artifice is an undertaking worse than academic.

The empty protest, whether political or artistic, has become a cliché. It has become the material for art or for a surrogate of art to such an extent that a book which did not contain some sort of denunciation would probably have no success today.

So we have an almost industrial market for alienation, that patent which no modern mind can do without. And observe this prudent hypocrisy: the solution to alienation and the consequent end of it are placed in a distant epoch, when a new social regeneration will be possible. Thanks to alienation everybody can believe in good faith that he desires liberty and that he has been deprived of it by forces greater than himself. And so man is spared the disconcerting discovery that he has never wanted to be free.

Man has never taken a decision on his own without a profound sense of unease. If anything comforts man it is the feeling of being moved, propelled. Historians, and above all certain philosophers, know this, for they believe that everything that happens is always right and what does not happen is always wrong. Only true scientists (and there are not many of them) know that if history is nature it does not point in any particular direction. If history is not nature, on the other hand, it is impossible to see how the reversal of nature or even the flouting of nature can take place. It is most unlikely that there can be any cohabitation or collaboration between two facts or entities which know nothing about each other.

But there is no point in saying that alienated man is no longer a man and that he is consequently incapable of expressing himself in a human way. If he has ceased to be a man he should not express himself in words but by other means and other activities, like a beaver or an ant. If, however, he is still a man, diminished though he be, he must attribute some significance to himself—a privilege which, in his own proud opinion, is denied to all other biologically living beings. Besides, if man is diminished, we again have the problem of commitment, of finding a way out, a problem which modern artists obviously cannot face without destroying their own basic premises.

To belong to a generation which can no longer believe in anything may be a cause of pride for anyone convinced of the ultimate nobility of this emptiness or of some mysterious need for it, but it does not excuse anyone who wants to transform this emptiness into a paradoxical affirmation of life simply in order to give himself a style. In a visual and spectacular society like ours, aesthetics have an incalculable importance.

Perhaps the day will come when only anthropologists and psychologists, not literary critics, will be able to say why the world of today, the whole world, no longer knows what to do with reason and liberty.

The interest aroused by the darkest millennia would be meaningless if it did not correspond to a profound need of our epoch. And if we look closely we can say that the hidden object of the new arts is to accelerate the approach of a time in which even the modern era, not to mention the ancient one, will become prehistoric.

Then, maybe, only the occasional scholar will see this immense amount of "research" as one of the most extraordinary aspects of the struggle of our time against Time.

The anti-work produced today is a contradiction in terms because, by destroying, it expresses a passionate and individualistic nostalgia for the closed work. But we must beware: the means that destroy choice and individual decision cannot be considered neutral or indifferent to their own content.

I do not think that the triumph of new technical means is altogether irrelevant in a world which inclines toward a positive and scientific humanism and tries to improve the lives of multitudes of men, but I do think that even tomorrow the most important voices will be those of the artists who, from their own isolation, echo the fatal isolation of each one of us. In this sense only those who are isolated speak. Only the isolated communicate. The others—the men of mass communication—repeat, echo, vulgarize the words of the poets. And although these are not words of faith today, they might well become so in the future.

There remains the hope that the art of the word, an incurably semantic art, will sooner or later make its repercussions felt even in those arts which claim to have freed themselves from every obligation toward the identification and representation of truth.

But it is precisely the semantic character of the word that creates obstacles which some people consider to be insuperable. And so, in the present state of art, the capacity to do without reason seems to be reserved for the visual and aural arts, while it is agreed, however reluctantly, that the artist of the word can still use reason. This situation will probably last a long time. There is nothing to make us believe that mass production may be slowing down. Books written in a comprehensible language run no risk for the time being; authors capable of making themselves understood will be able to go on giving us their works as they always have done.

This does not mean that they will escape the threat of increasing discredit.

Consequently, even in the art of the word we are witnessing the development of an ever greater inferiority complex.

Once we have discovered that the word is a sign, that the sign varies from context to context and can be analyzed in itself, not only does the language of the artist-writer become increasingly difficult, but criticism itself will not remain far behind. Many years ago it was decided that the history of poetry must be relegated to the kingdom of impossibility. But today the most the critic can do is to check certain linguistic results by using instruments taken from other sciences and disciplines, and he will not really be able to close his eyes to the precarious nature of verification processes which can themselves be destroyed by more up-to-date methods. In the end, reason will be an instrument reserved for critics and (anti-philosophical) philosophers, not a tool for artists. But what reason will the critics use? Whoever follows the reviews and publications of the young will see that the reasonings they contain will be incomprehensible in a few years' time. It is not that they were· wrong to start with: they will simply appear wrong for future readers because they try to judge rationally acts, gestures, and impulses which defy reason. So there is nothing to be done, and nothing can be done about it for many years to come. In the age of science and technology reason is towed along behind, and every effort is being made to pension it off.

One of the commonest aspects of commitment is of a linguistic nature. We must create a new language, and this is something we tend to do in bursts of enthusiasm, forgetting that such a reform takes place on its own, spontaneously, and that the real problem today would be to slow it down, if not actually to prevent it.

Once the problem of knowledge has been dismissed as anti-philosophical, we admit that things are what they are, defined by conventional words, and that behind things, behind man, we must not search for anything. Even the world is exactly what it is, what it seems to be, and we cannot do anything to modify it.

I do not know whether semiology will ever establish itself as a science. The very men who observe this discipline have difficulty in defining it because everything is a sign in the world of forms, sounds, and colors, and a science embracing everything remains inconceivable. But if we want to bide by verbal languages there are certainly considerable differences between the word as it is seen and the word as it is read and understood. The word as it is seen is far less alphabetical than the word as it is read and pronounced. It can be regarded as an ideogram.

Its faults are its lack of multivalence and its claim to some lasting truth. The industry of communication would be basically undermined if the various means of expression claimed to have any duration in time. What we need is not language but the suggestion, the arabesque, which is born and dies within a few minutes. What we need is that which we see, hear, and touch for a single moment, and which is then consumed and replaced by a similar stimulus.

The substitution of the word by something other than the word, by different means of expression, proves that man is tired of being man, and it is consequently perfectly logical that he should erase from what he produces any reference to the miserable human condition.

Why do poets no longer depict the human figure and the landscape in which man lives? Because, behind man and behind his real habitat, there always lies hidden the insidious word. A work of art which can be explained, translated in terms of language, still belongs to the old world which thought it could explain, justify, understand: it is a work that does not move, it is born old.

Once language has been reduced to a stammer and once it is admitted that it serves no more practical a purpose than that of a utilitarian sign, conversation becomes useless, and the affirmation of views which claim to crystallize the flux of life in one direction or another becomes ridiculous. What remains is the problem of communication, which is anything but insoluble on a practical level. One cannot communicate ideas but one can communicate facts and requirements with the art of the sign, the allusion, and the use of practical ciphers—and all this is provided for by the science of visual communications.

The almost total disappearance of conversation has caused the exchange of ideas to become a particular kind of spectacle. Three or four individuals who are considered qualified or in a position to express ideas meet at a round table, and a dazed and bored audience listens to them talking.

In the meantime, those who organize public life—politicians, administrators, business men—cannot appear with impunity to have no general ideas, no opinions. And the greater the reality of the void, the more they are obliged to conceal it with their verbosity. Nor could matters be otherwise since language—the vehicle of every opinion—is in a state of crisis. An important school of philosophy has tried to demonstrate that language does not grasp real entities: it only grasps phantoms. Man does not really know anything about himself, but in order to live he must give himself purely provisional meanings. The philosopher is aware of his ignorance, but it is essential to prevent the man in the street from discovering the ignorance of the intellectuals.

Can we prevent this? There was a time when we could because men of learning, supported by religion or by some positive philosophy, still had opinions, and above all because uneducated men were kept outside the realm of thought. Only very few men were authorized to think. The bomb of thought was guarded by a handful of specialists who did not have any interest in setting it off. Today, however, the bomb has exploded, and even the individual who is completely illiterate suspects that his ignorance is as valuable as the most sophisticated doctrine.

Consequently, that collective figure, which is always somewhat hypothetical but which is composed of real figures and calls itself "the public," has disappeared. There is no true profane public for art any more: there is only an enormous mass of connoisseurs, accomplices, active or potential artists. Within this mass some conflict can take place provided it does not undermine the general efficiency of the whole. Although this theory is not new in itself it turns art into a mere game.

There are no conspiracies; there is simply a spontaneous convergence of created interests. It is inevitable that cultural industry should invest not in its values, which are few, but in its non-values, which are many, aggressive, and prepared to disguise themselves in order to remain on the surface and be forever new and relevant.

We cannot even ask ourselves whether the human mind, so subdivided and pulverized, can still allow itself to be concentrated in some work or image of capital importance. In order to say that it can, we would

have to know whether the mind was a limited substance. If it was, and if it was meted out to everybody
in small doses, it would no longer permit the existence
of great masses and accumulations.

What animates man? Biology or dialectics? Neither the one nor the other offers him any consolation. Man is not particularly interested to know that one day he may well be able to create a facsimile of himself by artificial processes. He is far from interested in the discovery of new galaxies, and he is totally indifferent to the news that his mind contains a mechanism of theses, antitheses, and a final entity about which we know nothing.

But marvel, wonder, is the aim of all men, whether they are poets or not, and art is not a sum of figures to be added together: it is a leap, for quantities which do not belong to the same order cannot be totaled up.

Nor must we forget that art, in as much as it is a fashioned object, is also something physical, material. It is the creation of objects which did not exist before: it is not a language, or at least not a rational language.

The artists who endeavor to reproduce in their

anti-works the ebb and flow of a life in permanent transformation adopt a mimetic form of behavior which, in the best of cases, can be defined as reactionary. The identification of truth is different from the imitation of truth. We forget that art is not something natural.

In art it is not so much the rhetorical figures that count, the themes, motifs, messages (elements which are always the same and can even be enumerated) as it is their artificial representation. The artist disposes of a quantity of images, metaphors, patterns, procedures, and structures which have always been the same, ever since the times of the earliest fables. The problem of the creative artist is to make them appear to be something new despite the existence of an almost infinite number of precedents—for the series of combinations is inexhaustible. Indeed, it is precisely from the impact, from the contradiction, between old and new that art produces its most powerful themes. Nor must we think that the search for novelty is a mechanical process for the artist, like certain games which present us with a landscape reduced to microscopic fragments and which invite us to reconstruct a pre-existing original. The artist has no program or goal which can be defined from the start. What animates him is the sense of a void to be filled, the presentiment of a form which he will only know when it has been attained. And the instruments he uses are not gratuitous. They belong to a store which has always been at the disposal of men born to create. This store is the only true guarantee of forms which become his form when organized in a context within living history, and which then emerges from it provisionally. This is why the various elements which combine to constitute a work are merely contextual, and in this fact we can perceive the first seed of what was later to become the structuralist theory of art.

At all times art has presented us with the inviolable canon of an absolute unreality. Art begins where reality ends—of this Émile Zola, the great exaggerator of reality, was convinced. At the opposite pole we have Pushkin and Tolstoy, whose truths are too true to be credible. This is the miracle of an art which seems to be easy without being so and which cannot attain to art.

The artist's degree of self-awareness is never absolute and is often totally nebulous. And with what common code will we be able to decipher the mythopoetic manifestations of artists? Is there really a type of art whose death is "accepted" forever?

A *Weltanschauung* which turns the human being into a mere subjective illusion, a bad dream, raises the problem of killing new superstitions, no less terrible than the old ones, and above all the superstition that man can transcend his nature by agreeing to become the simple, undifferentiated part of a whole.

Art destined to last in time has the appearance of a natural truth, not of an experimental discovery performed in cold blood. The expansion of a reality which is known or about to be known demands the expansion of the sphere of comprehension and an inward growth of the artistic themes.

This is why most manifestations today cannot be judged. A scale of values would presuppose a link between the past and the future, a present full of antecedents and pointing surreptitiously to possible consequences. But this is not our real state since only the brief moment of the present seems to be the object of our knowledge.

Ever since poets have been following a poetic code which denies time and history and have aspired to the ultimate condition of absolute poetry (an aspiration of which by no means everyone is conscious) they have been placing themselves outside temporal history. And it is in an extra-temporal context that the so-called classics, both major and minor, are read today, as indeed are nearly all writers who require a considerable background knowledge and a great deal of concentration before they can be judged historically. Today we read a Greek fragment or a *dizain* by Maurice Scève as if we were reading a poem written yesterday. We read it in a flash of psychological time, which is far from that sense of time loaded with the past, of time contained and revived in ourselves, far, too, from that sense of eternal contemporaneity which a certain form of historicism taught us at a time when a philosophy still existed.

In the modern world, artists (millions of artists) are their own audience and their own judges. They do not need to delegate this power to anyone. Artists can proceed to self-government: the first and only self-government which has a definite chance of success.

All artists who have operated in the civilized world, from prehistory to the beginning of the twentieth century, have always committed the sin of mimesis. That is to say that they have described (or alluded to) something which transcended their own work. This "something" could be an entity or a reason which remained beneath the apparent meaning of the work and could be considered as an invariable opposed to or distinct from the mutability of the various forms created by artists. Even when the creators appeared to move away from close imitation of reality—the primitives, the Baroque artists, the romantics, the impressionists, etc.—the reference to the Eternal, the Immutable, may have become ever more remote, but it was always there. The concept of art, of "fine art," can also be used to define so-called classical art, which sanctions a provisional encounter between the real and the ideal but cannot bridge the fundamental gap. The vital works of today can no longer be regarded as artistic. Art is dead and is being substituted by a quiddity for which we will have to find another name.

And yet criticism seems to be the true literary genre of our time. There is no great critic, but there is an abundance of criticism. It is not really concerned with books—at best it is a chapter of cultural anthropology. It is essential for the market. It has lost its function as a post-factum judgment and is now becoming more and more an anticipatory, normative activity which provides artists with opinions and directions.

We no longer have to find a single image capable of defining poetry in a flash. The important advance—and we must take it into account—is that after studying the sign, the word, critics and students of literature should have become aware of the contextuality of the word and, instead of regarding the work of literature solely as a "machine made of words," they should regard it as a system of relationships whose center is everywhere and nowhere.

It is therefore not only on words that we should concentrate, but also on the main lines of a work in relation to their congruence to a whole, to a structure which is rightly identified by the critic, but one of which the author of the work may be totally unaware.

If this happens, if the poet does not have a clear awareness of the materials he is using, the much abhorred intuitive character of the work reappears when it should really remain hidden. But this is of no great importance. When it has been agreed, once and for all, that art does not know what art is, but that the discipline which studies this unknown substance is a real science, a rigorous science (though this appears to be most doubtful), we can make some concession to what little the ingenuous, or even the unconscious, mind suggests to whoever is creating a work in progress. Any further progress is not the task of the artist but of the scientist of this multiform yet no less existing material.

We can thus infer (as has already been done) that all that exists is the aesthetic experience which does not need absolute objects so much as relationships. It can perfectly well create its own objects without the assistance of any soi-disant "artists" or "works," but it simply cannot do without the interpreters of these provisional relationships, in other words the critics.

But I think that life has the meaning which we choose to impose on it—we, the men of knowledge and thought. Consequently, the world coincides with the definition which we (we who are authorized to think) will decide to give it. If those who interpret, or rather who invent, the mentality of the time, the breath of the

Zeitgeist, proclaim that good and evil, justice and injustice, are two insignia which are not complementary but interchangeable, then the world could end without anyone's noticing it, not only amongst psalmodies and jeremiads, but even accompanied by trumpet fanfares.

Let us also consider that good and evil are not machines, but that they are equally human creations. But we do not see how they can be guarded by men of culture reduced to stammering or silence.

We can consequently persist in thinking that the earthly adventure of man must have some sort of meaning. Reason may not be able to discern this meaning, yet it confirms its existence even when it imposes a limit on itself.

Evil, total emptiness, would result from the loss of the meaning and the memory of time which must flow into the time of tomorrow. It would be the cessation of this process, this scale of values which the great minds of the past tried to construct so that man—even alienated man—should create another image of his own earthly destiny.

Material needs, sacrosanct in themselves, can mask a form of impoverishment, if, when we give, we are merely removing something from others. Whatever is removed from the man of today—by every party, every technology, every conservativism or reformism or revolutionism—is no more nor less than love.

Poetry is one of the many positive possibilities of life.

For me the miracle is as obvious as the necessity.

Immanence and transcendence cannot be separated, and to think in terms of a perennial mediation between the two, as modern historicism has been suggesting, either does not resolve the problem or resolves it with an irremediable but joyless optimism.

I love the age in which I was born because I prefer to live in the stream rather than to vegetate in the marsh of an age without time.

Although I am not denying the infinite amount of impostures by which we are submerged, men seem to have opened their eyes wider today than they have ever done before, even in the age of Pericles. But their wide open eyes have not seen anything yet. We may have to wait a long time, and for me, as for all of us who are alive, time is running out.

But ideological commitment is not a necessary or an adequate condition for a poetically vital work. Nor is it, in itself, a negative condition. Every true poet has had his moment of commitment and has not waited for some obscure regulator or guide to give him his instructions.

Many will continue to think that art is a way of life for those who do not really live—a compensation or a surrogate. But this does not justify any deliberate ivory tower: a poet must not turn his back on life. It is life which contrives to elude the poet.

Selected Bibliography of
Criticism of Eugenio Montale's works
published in Britain and the United States
1936-1969

Selected Bibliography of
Criticism of Eugenio Montale's works
published in Britain and the United States
1936-1969

G. ALMANSI *Earth and Water in Montale's Poetry*, in "Forum for Modern Language Studies," II, 1966, pp. 377-85

ANON. *The Mediterranean Man*, "Times Literary Supplement," 28 *January 1965, p. 66* (Rev. of George Kay's English translation of Montale)

ANON. *Satura*, in "Times Literary Supplement," 30 July 1971, p. 890

C. B. BEALL *Quasimodo and Modern Poetry*, in "Northwest Review," IV, Eugene, Oregon, April-June 1961, pp. 41-48
—*Eugenio Montale's Warcofaghi'*, in "Linguistica and Literary Studies in Honor of H. A. Hatzfeld," Catholic University of America Press, Washington, 1964

IRMA BRANDEIS *Eugenio Montale*, in "Saturday Review of Literature," LXVI, 1, 18 July 1936, pp. 1-32
—(ed.) *Montale Issue*, "Quarterly Review of Literature," XI, 4, 1962

STANLEY BURNSHAW (ed.) *The Poem Itself*, World Publishing Co., Cleveland, Ohio, 1962, pp. 316-25

GLAUCO CAMBON *Eugenio Montale's Poetry: The Meeting of Dante and Bruegel*, in "Sewanee Review," LXVI, 1, 1958, pp. 1-32
—*Ungaretti, Montale and Lady Entrophy*, in "Italica," XXXVII, Nr. 4, Evanston, Illinois, 1960, pp. 231-38
—*The Garden of Apocalyptic Memory of Montale: A Biographical Note*, in "Quarterly Review of Literature," XI, Nr. 4, New York, 1962, pp. 288-94
—*The Privacy of Language: A Note on Eugenio Montale's "Obscurity,"* in "Modern Language Notes," LXXVII, Nr. 1, January 1963, pp. 75-9
—*Two Friendships*, in "Umanesimo," I, Nr. 2, 1966, pp. 22-9
—*Eugenio Montale's Motets: The Occasions of Epiphany*, in "PMLA," LXXXII, Nr. 7, 1967, pp. 471-84

—*Dante's Craft: Studies in Language and Style*, Minnesota University Press, Minneapolis, 1969, pp. 161-2

GIULIANA CAPRIOGLIO, *Intellectual and Sentimental Modes of Rapport with Reality in Montale's Ossi and Occasioni*, in "Italian Quarterly," LIX, 1969, pp. 50-66

D. S. CARNE-ROSS *A Master*, in "New York Review of Books," VIII, 20 October 1966, pp. 5-6

JOSEPH CARY *Three Modern Italian Poets: Saba, Ungaretti, Montale*, New York University Press, New York, 1969, pp. 235-327

J.M. CHOEN *Poetry of the Age*, London, 1960
—*Poetry of this Age: 1908-1965*, Hutchinson, London, 1966, pp. 128-32

GILBERT CREIGHTEN *The New Italian Writers*, in "Perspective," III, St. Louis, Missouri, Spring-Summer 1950

D. DELLA TERZA *Postwar Poetics and Poetry*, in "Italian Quarterly," IV, Nr. 13-14, 1960, pp. 39-49

O. EVANS *Three Modern Italian Poets (Saba, Montale, De Libero),* in "Voices" CXLV, Vinalhaven, Maine, May-August 1951, pp. 34-37

O. FORTI *Montale Within the Storm and Afterwards,* in "Umanesimo," 1, 2, 1966, pp. 1-14

H. FURST *The Literary Scene in Italy,* in "New York Times Book Review," 28 January 1940
(Favorable review of Montale's *Occasioni* considering him "one of the best living Italian poets.")

P. GATHERCOLLE *Two Kindred Spirits: Eugenio Montale and T. S. Eliot,* in "Italica," XXXII, 3, 1955, pp. 170-79

MICHAEL HAMBURGER *The Truth of Poetry: Tensions in Modern Poetry from Baudelaire to the Nineteen-sixties,* Harcourt Brace, New York, 1969, pp. 213-220

JAMES M. HERSEY *Eugenio Montale,* in "Bucknell Review," II, 1955
—*Eugenio Montale: The Analysis of a Few Poems in the Tradition of "The Waste Land,"* in "Bucknell Review," V, 1958

C. HUFFMAN *The Poetic Language of Eugenio Montale,* in "Forum Italicum," XII, Nr. 47-48, 1969, pp. 105-28

C. A. McCORMICK *Sound and Silence in Montale's Ossi di seppia,* in "Modern Language Review," LXII, 1967, pp. 633-41

DAVID NOLAN *Three Modern Italian Poets (Montale, Ungaretti, Quasimodo),* in "Studies," Spring 1969, pp. 61-72

SERGIO PACIFICI *Montale: The Quest for Meaning,* in "A Guide to Contemporary Italian Literature," World Publishing Co., Cleveland, Ohio, 1962, pp. 177-187

A. PELLEGRINI *A Letter from Italy,* in "Sewanee Review," 1951, pp. 700-722.

A. PIPA *The Message of Montale,* in "Italica," XXXIX, 4, 1962, pp. 239-55
—*Memory and Fidelity in Montale,* in "Italian Quarterly,"

39, 40, 1967, pp. 62-79

—*Montale and Dante*, University of Minnesota Press, Minneapolis, 1968

R. POGGIOLI *Italian Literary Chronicles: Poetry, 1944–47*, in "Italica," March 1948, p. 54

MARIO PRAZ *T. S. Eliot and Eugenio Montale*, in "T. S. Eliot, A Symposium," Poetry, London, 1948

M. S. SIMONELLI *The Particular Poetic World of Eugenio Montale*, in "Italian Quarterly," III, 10, 1959, pp. 41-53

G. S. SINGH *Eugenio Montale*, in "Italian Studies," XVIII, 1963, pp. 101-37

—*Eugenio Montale*, in "Books Abroad," 3, Oklahoma, 1966, p. 40

—*Eugenio Montale, Auto da fe*, in "Books Abroad," 1, Oklahoma, 1967, p. 41

—*Omaggio a Montale*, in "Modern Language Review," LXIV, 1, January 1969, pp. 190-192

—*Montale*, in "Times Literary Supplement," London, 12 June 1969

N. STOCK *Montale and Trakl*, in "Poetry Australia," 14, 1967, pp. 42-44

E. WILLIAMSON *Contemporary Italian Poetry*, in "Poetry," LXXXIX, Nr. 3, 1951, pp. 159-81, and Nr. 4, 1952, pp. 233-44

OTHER BOOKS OF INTEREST PUBLISHED BY URIZEN

LITERATURE

Ehrenburg, Ilya
The Life of the Automobile, novel,
   192 pages
Cloth $8.95 / paper $4.95

Enzensberger, Hans Magnus
Mausoleum, poetry, 132 pages
Cloth $10.00 / paper $4.95

Hamburger, Michael
German Poetry 1910-1975, 576 pages
Cloth $17.50 / paper $6.95

Handke, Peter
Nonsense & Happiness, poetry,
   80 pages
Cloth $7.95 / paper $3.95

Hansen, Olaf (Ed.)
*The Radical Will, Randolph Bourne
(Selected Writings) 1911-1918*
   500 pages
Cloth $17.50 / paper $7.95

Innerhofer, Franz
Beautiful Days, novel, 228 pages
Cloth $8.95 / paper $4.95

Kroetz, Franz Xaver
Farmyard & Other Plays, 192 pages
Cloth $12.95 / paper $4.95

Montale, Eugenio
Poet in Our Time (essays), 96 pages
Cloth $5.95 / paper $2.95

Shepard, Sam
*Angel City, Curse of the Starving
   Class, & Other Plays,* 300 pages
Cloth $15.00 / paper $4.95

FILM

Bresson, Robert
Notes on Cinematography, 132 pages
Cloth $6.95 / paper $2.95

Bresson, Robert
The Complete Screenplays, Vol. I,
   400 pages
Cloth $17.50 / paper $6.95

PSYCHOLOGY

Borneman, Ernest (Ed.)
The Psychoanalysis of Money, 420 pages
Cloth $15.00 / paper $5.95

Doerner, Klaus
Madmen and the Bourgeoisie, 384 pages
Cloth $15.00 / paper $5.95

Patrick C. Lee and Robert S. Stewart
Sex Differences, 500 pages
Cloth $17.50 / paper $5.95

Moser, Tilman
Years of Apprenticeship on the Couch,
240 pages / Cloth $10.00

ECONOMICS

De Brunhoff, Suzanne
Marx on Money, 192 pages
Cloth $10.00 / paper $4.95

Linder, Marc
Anti-Samuelson Vol. I, 400 pages
Cloth $15.00 / paper $5.95
Anti-Samuelson, Vol. II, 440 pages
Cloth $15.00 / paper $5.95

SOCIOLOGY

Andrew Arato/Eike Gebhardt (Eds.)
The Essential Frankfurt School Reader,
544 pages / Cloth $17.50 / paper $5.95

Pearce, Frank
Crimes of the Powerful, 176 pages
Paper $4.95

Van Onselen, Charles
Chibaro (African Mine Labor in Southern
Rhodesia), 368 pages / Cloth $17.50

Shaw, Martin
Marxism Versus Sociology
   (A Reading Guide), 120 pages
Cloth $6.95 / paper $2.25

Shaw, Martin
Marxism and Social Science, 125 pages
Paper $2.95

Thönnessen, Werner
The Emancipation of Women, 185 pages
Cloth $10.00 / paper $4.95

Write for a complete catalog to:
Urizen Books, Inc., 66 West Broadway, New York, N.Y. 10007

42 9
275
‾‾‾‾‾‾
2|4 5
  3